Chapter 1

Preparing the Foundations

◆

This chapter sets the foundation for developing assertive behavior and learning the different styles of communication: *passive, passive/aggressive, aggressive,* and *assertive.*

There are two main tasks here. First, identify your style of communication:

◆ passive

◆ passive/aggressive

◆ aggressive

◆ assertive

Second, know your worth:

◆ Understand yourself.

◆ Accept and forgive yourself for the way you are.

◆ Decide to change—*if you want to*.

◆ Give yourself permission to succeed—*and to fail*.

IDENTIFY YOUR STYLE OF COMMUNICATION

In order to understand ourselves, and why we don't behave assertively, we must first examine our current *patterns of behavior*. We will not dwell on our failures; we will merely use them for information and for our motivation to change.

Note your behavioral pattern, in both your personal and professional lives. It is this that determines the way people respond to you and it is this in turn that determines the outcome of all your communication.

If you have difficulty identifying the pattern in yourself, ask a friend to help—but remember, they are doing you a favor.

For instance: are you very aggressive, uncompromising, fixed in your views, intolerant, or impatient? Are you sarcastic, manipulative, dismissive, arrogant or superior? Are you acquiescent, apologetic, deferring, or self-effacing?

It is interesting to note that most people who want to develop assertive behavior fit into the last category—that of victim.

People always treat you the way you ask to be treated. Understanding what you are asking for is half the battle. You are now in a position to observe yourself carefully and honestly, and to make the changes that *will* make the changes.

Don't feel hopeless at this point; from now on, everything is a positive step.

Remember: All it takes to change is a decision.

Most people's behavior patterns demonstrate some characteristics from each of the four categories just noted—*passive, passive/ aggressive, aggressive,* and *assertive*—depending on the circumstances of the communication. However, one category will most likely dominate your style. Read through the descriptions below and see which one holds true for you most of the time.

PASSIVE

Passive behavior is usually associated with the loser—one who is always backing down, giving in, and being submissive. Apologies are rife in this mode of communication, as are reluctant agreements and negative statements about the self. Passive behavior conveys the message "you're OK, I'm not OK."

PASSIVE/AGGRESSIVE

Passive/aggressive behavior is usually associated with the saboteur. It is by no means overt, but the aggressive motivation is obvious nonetheless. The distinguishing features of this mode of communication are sarcastic comments, comments with double meanings, and nonverbal signals such as mockingly gazing heavenwards. The underlying message is "I'm not OK, you're not OK."

AGGRESSIVE

Aggressive behavior takes no account of the rights of others. Although this person may be perceived to be a go-getter or one of life's winners, she is usually feared and her style encourages deceitful behavior from others who would rather not face up to the aggressor's wrath. The message conveyed by this person is "I'm OK, you're not OK."

ASSERTIVE

Assertive communication does not diminish or put down another human being, it does not trespass on any human rights and it does not shy away from important issues. Rather, it encourages satisfactory communication where everyone's needs are met in the best way. The identifying characteristic of assertive behavior is the use of "I" statements. This indicates that the person communicating is taking responsibility for the message that is being conveyed. For example, "I am not happy with this decision, I would like to discuss it further." This form of communication is based on respect for self and others. It is driven by the belief that "I'm OK, you're OK." There are no losers.

A word of caution. Assertive behavior does not necessarily mean that you get your way all the time. It *does* mean that the chances of getting to the best solution, with everyone's self-esteem intact, are significantly enhanced.

The main characteristic associated with each style of communication follows. If you have difficulty determining whether you are passive, passive/aggressive, assertive, or aggressive, you may be able to identify with one of these characteristics instead. You can then find your dominant style by reading the definition below each.

Surrendering	Undermining	Facilitating	Argumentative
☐	☐	☐	☐
Passive	Passive/ Aggressive	Assertive	Aggressive

This should give you an idea of where the work on your communication skills should begin.

If you fall naturally into the passive category, you will most probably be eager to change your behavior to the more assertive type. You will recognize that the adoption of this style of communication will mean that you can, at last, stop undermining and diminishing yourself. It holds many rewards for you.

If however, you fall into the aggressive category, it will be hard for you to move into assertive behavior because it will feel as if you are losing control. Be brave; you are actually *gaining* control and winning commitment from those communicating with you.

For those of you who are passive/aggressive, at the moment you are actually letting *others* determine how you feel. You probably expect them to guess your feelings, feel sorry for causing them, and change their behavior towards you. It would be far less stressful to start taking control and start making your own choices.

If you are still unsure of your dominant style of communicating behavior, work through the simple questionnaire on pages 7 and 8. Do not worry if your responses fall into all the different categories; identify with the strongest trend. The mix of responses will help you focus on the specific areas in your style that you may wish to change.

It really doesn't matter how you label yourself as long as you know what your objectives are.

Broadly speaking, if most of your responses fall into the Sometimes category, you tend to be aggressive or passive/aggressive. If they fall into the Never category you are certainly passive. If you find that your responses are predominantly in the Often column, you are well on the way to being assertive.

Communication Style Questionnaire

	Sometimes	Often	Never
1 I feel that I represent myself well in all communications	☐	☐	☐

	Sometimes	Often	Never
2 My ideas are considered valuable and often adopted	☐	☐	☐
3 My opinions are sought by others	☐	☐	☐
4 I am able to make complaints and am satisfied with the outcome	☐	☐	☐
5 I am able to criticize another without causing offense	☐	☐	☐
6 I can communicate effectively in a group	☐	☐	☐
7 I am able to ask for help	☐	☐	☐
8 I am able to meet my own needs	☐	☐	☐
9 I control my temper	☐	☐	☐
10 People find that I am good at talking through ideas and problems	☐	☐	☐
11 I am free from disabling stress	☐	☐	☐
12 I feel comfortable with who I am	☐	☐	☐

KNOW YOUR WORTH

UNDERSTAND YOURSELF
We all have basic human rights:

◆ the right to choose

◆ the right to be

◆ the right to be respected

◆ the right to make mistakes

◆ the right to say no

◆ the right to ask for what we want

◆ the right to ask for what we need

It is *always* our fears that block us from developing assertive behavior. What are yours?

"I will lose my friends," "I will make a fool of myself," "No one will like me any more," "I will become irritating,". . . (fill in your own).

Our fears are *always* larger than reality. Face them; they have a wonderful habit of shrinking.

ACCEPT AND FORGIVE YOURSELF FOR THE WAY YOU ARE

It is very easy to put yourself down. We are our own worst critics.

It is helpful to know that we are:

◆ *what* we are supposed to be;

◆ *where* we are supposed to be;

◆ *doing what* we are supposed to do.

Release all your disappointments and guilts—forgive yourself. Everything that you have done and experienced has brought you to this point of change.

DECIDE TO CHANGE—IF YOU WANT TO

In making your decision to change your behavior, you may find it helpful to project forward in time and imagine how it would look, and feel, if you were in control of your communication. Compare this to how you feel now.

The power of imaging or visualizing cannot be overstressed. It is a very useful tool for achieving your objectives, whatever they are.

By bringing to mind or picturing in your mind's eye your desired state, you are actually putting images into your subconscious mind that ultimately determine your behavior. Your subconscious mind can only work in images, it does not understand timescales or conditions. Imagine yourself as you would like to be and your subconscious will work tirelessly to make this a reality. It cannot fail. Keep reinforcing the images time after time, using positive affirmations if this helps (see Chapter 2 for more on this), and the old patterns will soon be obliterated and replaced with the new ones that you have chosen.

Old habits die hard, but they do die if you are persistent and determined to change.

If you continue to behave as you have always behaved, people will continue to treat you as they have always treated you.

GIVE YOURSELF PERMISSION TO SUCCEED—AND TO FAIL

You are embarking on a journey of transformation. It will not always be easy but it will be rewarding.

There will be times when you don't do a thing wrong. Your communication with others will be assertive and effective and you will be amazed at how differently you are perceived. There will also be times when you slip back into your old habits.

All this is part of your learning. Don't beat yourself up when you fail. You will be grateful for all these experiences sometime in the future when it really matters.

By now you should have identified your dominant style of communication and decided whether or not you are completely happy to continue in this vein.

If you decide to make changes in the way you communicate and in the way you are perceived by your colleagues, then proceed with enthusiasm; there is much you can gain from the following chapters.

SUMMARY

To recap, the different communication styles are broadly divided into the following categories:

◆ passive

◆ passive/aggressive

◆ assertive

◆ aggressive

These are loosely associated with the following characteristics:

◆ victim

◆ manipulator

◆ achiever

◆ dictator

Chapter 2

Creating Winning Scenarios

◆

This chapter will bring us a little bit closer to being in control of our lives—asserting ourselves in the way we choose. We will look at:

◆ winning language

◆ positive affirmations

◆ creative visualization

◆ building self-esteem

Those who are adept at turning on assertive behavior are also quite able to observe their actions, talk themselves through their learning, and test the effect of new behaviors. Self-knowledge is the key to taking control of our lives.

Observing, questioning, and asking for feedback is vital if we are to succeed.

WINNING LANGUAGE

Winning language is the language of assertive behavior. It speaks more than words to those you communicate with and tells them that you are in control.

Those who recognize this quality in you will nonetheless be hard pressed to say exactly what it is that you are doing to give them this impression. Actually, it is a subtle combination of body language, mental attitude, and verbal language.

Remember: *It's not what you say that counts, it's the way you say it.*

The winning qualities of an assertive communicator are:

◆ direct, clear language

◆ an ability to demonstrate understanding and to empathize (active listening skills)

◆ an ability to build rapport and maintain relationships

◆ good posture, voice, and eye contact

◆ confidence in what you say—no self-effacing comments or profuse apologies!

Let's look at these qualities in more detail.

DIRECT CLEAR LANGUAGE

Language can be a very inadequate and clumsy tool for communication. It can also be beautifully simple and, combined with reinforcing body language, can be extremely effective and evocative.

Here are some simple rules to help you practice assertive, winning, language:

◆ *Set the scene* by describing—very briefly—what you are referring to: "When you called a meeting last Friday, I . . . "

◆ *Simplicity, clarity, and brevity* are key to assertive communication. Do not ramble; you will lose the attention of your audience. Make your point quickly.

◆ *Take responsibility* for what you are saying. This is done by using "I" statements. Here are two examples of "I" statements; one negative and one positive: "I am unhappy about the way this project is proceeding." "I'm delighted with the outcome of this meeting."

◆ *Use repetition* if you feel that your message isn't getting across, but restructure your statement the second time.

◆ *Use silence appropriately*–it can say more than words. Don't be afraid of it; try it out.

ACTIVE LISTENING SKILLS

Active listening ranks high on the totem pole of the various communication skills. It enables you to empathize with your audience and build successful relationships.

Good listeners do several things when communicating. They:

◆ *paraphrase*—briefly summarize what has just been said;

◆ *ask open questions* to elicit good information—*how* and *what* (*why* can sound whiney or inquisitorial);

◆ *show an interest*—maintain good eye contact and prompt more communication by nodding from time to time, using encouraging words like *yes*, *aha*, and *mmm*;

◆ *give feedback*—reflect back what they believe is being said.

BUILDING RAPPORT AND MAINTAINING RELATIONSHIPS

Everybody needs to feel liked and valued, and they will be generous in their dealings with you if you manage to develop a healthy rapport. It is a good investment *if done genuinely and generously*. If you do this as a manipulative technique, your motivation will almost certainly be exposed.

Developing true rapport is based on taking an interest in the other party, understanding and remembering what they have said, and remembering to acknowledge significant events or achievements.

Body language also plays a part in developing rapport (more about this in Chapter 6).

It sometimes helps to write down others' activities as well as your own if you are forgetful. However, you will soon learn that if you manage to develop active listening skills and build empathetic relationships, you will start to remember things more reliably. This is because you will have been concentrating on what the other person has been saying, and you will have heard yourself summarize the main points.

Hearing yourself say something really does help you to remember. *Talking to yourself is not a sign of madness; it is a valuable aid to the memory.*

GOOD POSTURE, VOICE, AND EYE CONTACT

It is somewhat galling to note that only about 7 percent of what you say (the words you use) contributes towards the message you are trying to convey.

Much more of the message—38 percent—is carried in your voice. This includes tone, pitch, speed, and the quality of your voice.

The remainder, some 55 percent, is conveyed by your body. This, of course, is why the telephone can be so misleading. Messages have a tendency to become distorted when confined to only two of the three channels of communication available to you (words and voice, with no visible channel).

A large proportion of the messages you convey with your body are carried in the face, and more specifically, the eyes.

Good posture and an upright walk looks good and conveys confidence. Slouching or shuffling along gives completely the opposite impression. Try walking towards yourself in front of a mirror or catch a glimpse of yourself in a shop window. Notice the difference when you actively try to improve the way you move.

Assertive body language will be covered more fully in Chapter 6, but there are several simple rules to consider for the time being:

◆ *Stand or sit proudly*—taking up as little space as possible conveys lack of confidence or weakness.

◆ *Gesture appropriately*—gestures can help in the understanding of a message when used sensibly. Try not to overdo it, however; a lot of extravagant gesturing can be very distracting.

◆ *Don't fidget*—this will make you appear nervous, as you probably are if you are fidgeting.

The use and quality of your *voice* and the way sound resonates around the bone structure of your face will contribute to the other person's perception of what you are saying.

A high-pitched, whiney voice, for example, which for some of us is our natural style, conveys a victim message: "I'm really rather weak and pathetic and I'm throwing myself on your mercy!" (Note how assertively this message is being conveyed—lots of I statements!) This style of voice can also sound spoiled and petulant.

By contrast, a loud, deep voice delivering words like machine gun fire sounds incredibly aggressive.

Notice your own dominant style. Would you like to change it?

The optimum style—if there is such a thing—is pitched mid-range with good intonation, clearly enunciated words, and a calm pace. It's not always appropriate, of course, but most of the time it will serve you well.

To communicate assertively, you must maintain good *eye contact.* Aim to maintain almost consistent eye contact while you are listening to another person. It is not so easy, indeed it can be disconcerting, to maintain constant eye contact while you are talking. Your eyes will help in the expression of your message and will no doubt be on the move much of the time. However, return your glance regularly to your subject throughout your talk; it will help you pick up how the other person is feeling about what you are saying.

It is worth noting that if your body is out of synchronization with your words, your hidden agenda will immediately be revealed—if not precisely what it is, at least the fact that you have one!

CONFIDENCE IN WHAT YOU SAY

Confidence is fine if you have it, but most unassertive people are sadly lacking in this department. However, here are some useful tips that you can learn to incorporate in your repertoire very easily.

◆ *Say what you mean and mean what you say*—be succinct and use the "I" statement.

◆ *Never apologize*—unless you sincerely mean it, then only do it once.
(Notice how politicians and business leaders almost *never* apologize. Are we really convinced that they *never* make mistakes?)

◆ *Don't claim to be a fool* to compensate for feeling like a fool. We often do this to prompt a contradiction. One of the dangers of this strategy is that you will be believed.

POSITIVE AFFIRMATIONS

Used in the right way, positive affirmations can be enormously helpful. They retrain the brain to think about ourselves differently.

If we have a poor self-opinion (usually as a result of childhood experiences), then as soon as we suffer a loss of confidence, we return to this level of negativity. It takes repeated effort to over-come this tendency and to replace it with something more positive.

For some people, positive affirmations can be very helpful in this process.

Positive affirmations are constant repetitions of a belief we wish to install in our brains to replace the less healthy beliefs we have grown up with.

They must be constantly repeated to be effective. Think how long you have lived with your negativity, and then think how often you will have to repeat a desired belief before it will outweigh, and tri-umph over, the negative belief that is so firmly lodged in your brain.

Every time we have a thought, an electrical impulse sets off along a particular route through the brain. After this same thought has been thought many times, a physical path becomes etched in the brain. This will deepen with every thinking of the thought. If this happens to be a negative or undermining thought, it will color what you pro-ject to others. A new path must be created, therefore, that is even deeper, and therefore easier, for the thought to follow—the path of least resistance. This can be achieved through positive affirmations.

Say your positive affirmations every day, like a mantra, and even-tually you will find that you have reprogrammed your brain and installed a healthier belief.

There are several rules for designing positive affirmations.

◆ They must be in the present—"I am . . ."

◆ They must *not* be conditional—"When I . . . then I will . . ."

◆ They must *not* be undermined—hidden message: "Who am I trying to fool with all this stuff anyway?!"

◆ They must be about *you*, nobody else.

◆ They must be spoken *out loud*—in private if you wish, but it is important to *hear* yourself say them.

Examples of good affirmations are:

◆ "I can handle it."

◆ "I am professionally competent."

◆ "I am a valuable and capable member of the team."

CREATIVE VISUALIZATION

Creative visualization is an extremely powerful technique for seeing and fixing your far-distant goals in your mind's eye and for planning and rehearsing the tasks that will lead to achieving your goals.

The subconscious mind works in images, and when these are clear, it will work tirelessly to turn these images into reality.

What you need for effective creative visualization is a starting point and an end point. That is to say, you need to understand your current situation completely and notice how far away you are from reaching your goal.

This is not a negative exercise, it is an unemotional and nonjudgmental appraisal, to enable you to take realistic and positive action.

Once you have isolated and fully understood your current situation, you must then form a very clear image of your goal and see, feel, and sense it in your mind. Imagine it from a detached point of view, as if you were watching a film, and imagine it as if you were actually there, participating in it or living with it. Imagine it every way you can until you have a precise picture. Do not dismantle that picture; hold it clearly in your mind. Return to it regularly so that it becomes reinforced, time and again.

Set some time aside for this visualization so that you can build its strength over time. Do not try to hurry the achievement of your goal. Your subconscious will take the strain between your current situation and your desired state and will work to transform the first image into the second.

This method of achieving what you desire is infallible when done diligently. Indeed, you will probably have some personal experience of a time when you did this instinctively when you desired something so badly, and so clearly, that you managed to bring it to reality.

Try it with big desires and small, but make sure that they are yours and not anyone else's. You will not be able to use it to manipulate others to do what you want!

In summary, here are the basic steps to effective creative visualization—a method that many successfully assertive people adopt without even thinking about it.

◆ Develop a clear image of your goal.

◆ Breathe it, feel it, smell it, examine it from all angles.

◆ Notice your current situation and your distance from the goal.

◆ Plan and execute your first and second steps only.

◆ Do something else and leave your subconscious to work on the next stage undisturbed. Do not interfere, and do not undermine your images.

◆ The next steps will come to you in their own time.

◆ Return to reinforce the image of your goal and your current position regularly but infrequently.

◆ Trust the process; it will work.

Planning and rehearsing the tasks that have to be performed before reaching your goal are like mini creative visualizations. Each step can be treated in the same way as those listed above for a major goal. Never plan more than two steps ahead, however, as the path your subconscious mind leads you down may be different from the one you expect. Follow it: it will probably be more creative and more effective.

If you have no clear idea of the tasks, don't worry; they will pop into your mind when the moment is right.

When you have executed the tasks in your mind's eye, you will find that the ease with which you perform them in reality will be truly remarkable.

Once you have a clear idea of your goal, everything you do and every decision you make will be in the context of this goal.

BUILDING SELF-ESTEEM

Self-esteem, as opposed to ego, is very difficult to recapture once it is lost. Self-esteem is a measure of how you value yourself, and it is built up from your first breath—or, as in many cases, it is destroyed by damaging relationships. It is one of the most helpful personal qualities that you can possess, because from it stems the belief that you are worthy to succeed.

Sometimes people try to camouflage their low self-esteem by portraying excessive confidence. This is just "noise" used to mask their heartfelt feelings of vulnerability and inadequacy. Don't be fooled or intimidated by this. Recognize it as a human solution to intolerable emotional discomfort. In this way, the threat of what appear to be very confident people will disappear and you will be able to meet them on an equal footing.

Using some of the techniques described in this chapter can help to build self-esteem and confidence, but there is no substitute for knowing yourself and knowing the areas in which you are most likely to excel. There is nothing so powerful as a series of successes to lead you towards the establishment of a healthy self-esteem, so plan for them.

Here are some thoughts for you to consider when trying to raise the level of your self-esteem:

◆ Let go of being responsible for those around you: take responsibility for your own choices and feelings.

◆ Don't take yourself too seriously—once you lose your sense of humor, you have lost control.

◆ Have realistic expectations of yourself: do not compare yourself to an ideal—you will always fall short.

◆ Let go of your irrational self-perceptions—in your rational mind you will know what these are.

◆ Know yourself; understand what is blocking your progress—usually fear of failure, or guilt that you are not good enough.

◆ Nurture yourself—give yourself treats.

SUMMARY

This chapter offered some techniques that will enable you to be successfully assertive and to be in charge of your actions. Don't diminish the importance of these tools. If you practice them often they will become second nature to you.

Soon your colleagues will notice that you are more decisive, effective, and confident. This is excellent news for those who are managing or leading a team.

Remember:

Project a positive image by:

◆ adopting winning language

◆ using body language to reinforce your messages

◆ developing a positive mental attitude

◆ listening actively

◆ building rapport through empathy

All this will lead to:

◆ a healthy self-esteem

Please note, there is no danger of training your personality out of yourself. Your personal style will continue to distinguish you among your colleagues, even if they too are successful at being assertive. Indeed, you will feel freer to express yourself individually as you become more comfortable with your powers of assertion.

Chapter 3

Dealing with Negative Communication

◆

This chapter will help you negotiate your way through the most difficult territory in communication terms—that which is negative:

◆ handling anger—yours and others'

◆ resolving conflict

◆ giving and receiving criticism

◆ saying no

◆ handling rejection and failure

HANDLING ANGER—YOURS AND OTHERS'

Most of us nurse an innate fear of anger. This may be a throwback to our childhood years when we felt powerless and vulnerable. When we encounter anger, therefore, our bodies tend to react by preparing us for the fight-or-flight response—rapid heartbeat, rapid breathing, an increased supply of blood to the muscles—all as a result of the release of adrenalin into the bloodstream. This response is the natural defense mechanism that kicks in when we are threatened, and, at the right time, it is a lifesaver.

In most modern situations, however, this reaction is both inappropriate and unhelpful, and we must learn to override this natural tendency by reducing our fear. This may be achieved by understanding anger.

Anger is just energy. It can be directed by an angry person indiscriminately at things or specifically at you. It is like a heat-seeking missile looking for a target and it merely needs to be deflected or damped.

The thing to remember about anger is that it is not *you*, the personality, that has precipitated the anger, but some action or stance that you have taken that has struck an unhappy chord with the other. *You* are still an acceptable human being with rights. The anger you are fielding has arisen as a result of the other person's conditioning—sometimes unreasonable conditioning. The same is true of your anger, of course.

The best method for dealing with another's anger—in all but the pathological cases—is first to remove your personal investment in the situation. View it dispassionately from a distance and observe its nature while letting it burn itself out. Don't fuel it.

Try to identify the source of the anger by listening carefully to what is being said or shouted. You may find that the angry person feels criticized, unimportant, thwarted, hurt—any number of emotions. This will give you a clue as to how to proceed.

If you are still struggling, ask questions to clarify your understanding, but try not to be patronizing or unctuous.

If you are in a public place and you feel embarrassed, just remember that you are the one in control at the moment and that it is the other party that is drawing attention to himself—and he will, of course; we are a sensation-seeking society.

Once the heat has died down, communicate your understanding of the situation from the other's point of view and negotiate a way forward or a resolution.

If you feel that it is important to douse the anger rapidly, a useful technique to adopt is to match the energy being expended. This is done by making a loud proclamation such as "I UNDERSTAND WHY YOU ARE SO UPSET and I would feel exactly the same if I were you, but . . ." As you proceed, you can drop the pitch of your voice and start to take control.

As an observer, you can often hear when the heat is rising in a situation because voices tend to increase in pitch. Voices become high and whiney and words are delivered like machine gun fire. This is counter to all hope of control.

Try not to be tempted to use reason. The purpose of reasoning is to get the other to agree that their behavior is unreasonable, and nobody wants to do that when they are at fever pitch. This will obviously build resentment. Reasoning can be a passive/aggressive stance as it attempts to lure the other into a submissive position.

REMEMBER: YOU ALWAYS HAVE THE OPTION TO WALK AWAY.

When you feel angry yourself, try the distancing technique. (Deep breathing or counting to ten helps some people.) You can observe your own behavior quite dispassionately with practice. The observations you make of yourself will contribute enormously to your self-knowledge if you can do it honestly. You will reap untold rewards in your ability to communicate assertively.

Here is a checklist for helping you to cope with anger:

◆ Distance yourself; don't take anger personally.

◆ Understand the cause of the anger by listening and observing carefully.

◆ Say nothing until the anger has died down.

◆ Use a low-pitched voice and speak clearly.

◆ Respect yourself and the other party; you still both have rights.

◆ Once a certain degree of tranquillity has been achieved, demonstrate understanding by acknowledging the other's viewpoint (not the same thing as agreeing with it).

◆ Negotiate a way forward.

◆ If all else fails, walk away. This is another way of respecting yourself.

RESOLVING CONFLICT

For the purposes of clarity, conflict is treated as a separate entity from anger, although one can sometimes lead to the other.

Conflict can be invisible, insidious, and elusive, particularly with those of the passive/aggressive persuasion. It can lead to an impasse, a block that is extremely difficult to move. Many such conflicts and unresolved disputes in business lead to the destruction of an organization.

Conflict can also be clear, reasonable, and helpful. Used positively, it can sharpen the mind, increase understanding, and lead towards a very satisfying and creative solution.

Many of the techniques for dealing with conflict are similar to those used for dealing with anger. The issues may be more complex because the two opposing positions are often well thought out and rehearsed in advance. The goals of the two parties may at first appear totally different and incompatible. This is rarely the case in reality, however.

Here is a checklist for resolving conflict:

◆ Establish the desired outcome and priorities for both parties.

◆ Acknowledge and appreciate the other's position.

◆ Discuss the points of mutual agreement to establish rapport.

◆ Compromise on issues that are not central to the desired outcome.

◆ Identify and clarify those points that are left unresolved.

◆ Delve for deeper understanding by questioning thoroughly and listening carefully.

◆ Negotiate a resolution or agree on a plan for the next step.

GIVING AND RECEIVING CRITICISM
This is always difficult territory. We usually give criticism badly because we are not very good at receiving it.

GIVING CRITICISM
Giving early critical feedback prevents a bad situation from developing into a dreadful one.

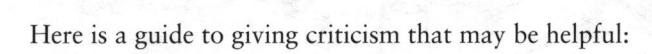

Here is a guide to giving criticism that may be helpful:

◆ Be considerate and, above all, be private.

◆ Don't pussyfoot around; have confidence in what you want to say (use I statements).

◆ Take responsibility for the criticism; don't do it because you have been cajoled into doing so, and don't base it on rumor.

◆ Make sure the criticism is based on the behavior you would like to see changed, not on the personality of the individual being criticized.

◆ Use positive body language (see Chapter 6).

Constructive criticism is often referred to as feedback and may be given following what is called a positive stroke. For instance: "I liked the way you handled that call, but it might portray better customer service if you used her name."

RECEIVING CRITICISM

None of us enjoys being criticized. Indeed, most of us are looking for a confirmation that we are liked and accepted the way we are. However, if we put our vulnerabilities behind us for a moment, it really can be very helpful to hear how others perceive our behavior or our work. We are then in a better position to make the desired adjustments, if we feel that they are valid.

Sometimes we may feel that criticism is unfair. If this is the case, try to retain every vestige of dignity possible, state your disagreement, and move on. Try not to argue for yourself; you will not convince anybody and you will hand your power straight to the person doing the criticizing.

Here is a quick checklist for receiving criticism:

◆ Attend carefully to what is being said.

◆ Judge for yourself if it is valid; if not, disregard it and move on.

◆ Do not argue; you will only draw attention to your vulnerabilities.

If you are unfortunate enough to be criticized in public, a dignified reaction will elicit a disproportionate amount of respect from observers while the standing of the person doing the criticizing will be severely diminished.

SAYING NO

We are rewarded with masses of praise when we acquiesce. This is not surprising as, in doing so, we have taken responsibility for somebody else's task or burden. By comparison, the emotional reward for saying no is somewhat barren.

We are often made to feel guilty and mean, even criticized. This is a form of manipulation, a last-ditch attempt to make you change your mind and cooperate after all.

Dealing with this requires a particular kind of resilience. It helps if you really do believe that it is perfectly acceptable to make choices according to your set of priorities, values, and beliefs. This does not mean that you need always say no just to prove that you are in control of your decisions. What it does mean is that you *can* say no.

Here is a list of useful tips that you can use when you want to say no:

◆ Really mean it —if you don't it will probably show and the person making the request will probe and pry until you change your mind.

◆ If you want to think about your response, say, "I will get back to you" or "I need some time to think about this." This is your right—who is doing who the favor?

◆ Don't milk the apology, wring your hands anxiously, or overplay the excuses.

◆ You may be able to offer a compromise solution.

HANDLING REJECTION AND FAILURE

It is very difficult to separate rejection and failure because they are so intrinsically linked.

They can bring utter despair and dejection, a feeling of foolishness, of being unworthy, and so many other negative emotions.

Accepting that this is the case for so many of us, the healthy thing to do is to learn from these emotions, work with them and view them from a more positive perspective. This may sound trite and unproductive, but with a bit of determination your perceived failures and consequent feelings of rejection will turn into humorous anecdotes.

"Did I tell you about the time when I asked the chairman if he was authorized to be in the building?"

Try not to confuse your true self-worth with one fleeting, albeit negative, experience. To be too harsh on yourself is unproductive and at a time like this, you need all the forgiveness and understanding you can get, even if it has to come from you.

One useful tactic you may like to employ to avoid the feeling of total defeat is to make a series of contingency plans. In thinking through possible, probable, or even improbable scenarios that are likely to tarnish your reputation, you can spend some useful time preparing coping strategies. In this way, you can redeem yourself rapidly and divert the destructive feelings of rejection and failure into a more positive arena.

However, don't dwell for too long on the negative; you may find you have creatively visualized something you would rather not come true.

These tips may be helpful as part of your survival package:

◆ Try not to link your own worth to a negative experience.

◆ Never be bereft of alternatives—develop contingency plans.

◆ Be kind to yourself.

◆ Know that the significance of negative experiences changes with time.

◆ Try to distill some learning from the experience—it will protect you next time.

The whole gamut of negative experiences and emotions are uncomfortable at best. But having conquered your fear and having successfully dealt with a few difficult situations, you will soon reeducate your reflex reactions to cooperate with the way you would rather be.

Developing a balanced view on these matters will make you much stronger because you won't be trying to avoid issues; instead you will be making choices and following them through confidently.

A word of caution. You are not invincible, so try not to get overzealous in your enthusiasm to tackle negativity. There definitely are situations that are best avoided because there can be no victor in their resolution. Anger that turns to physical violence is an irrational act and therefore cannot be approached in a rational way. In these circumstances, self-preservation is the key and if your body prepares you for flight, do it!

SUMMARY
In summary, what we have been dealing with today is negative energy. When this is understood, fear can evaporate, and this energy can be transformed into a positive outcome—positive for everyone.

Being able to identify with another human being caught in the grip of fury may enable us to empathize with his plight, and in so doing enable us to behave generously.

It is worth noting that behaving assertively, as you would be if you managed to control an angry exchange without destruction to either party's ego, is not always what you wish to achieve. Sometimes you may choose a good fight; so SHOUT BACK IF YOU WANT TO SHOUT BACK, but be sure you are doing this because you really want to and be sure to enjoy every moment of it. This is honoring yourself. But you may have to be prepared to pick up the pieces of your relationship later.

As an alternative, walk away if you want to walk away.

Chapter 4

Creating a Positive Impression in the Private Arena

♦

There are many possibilities for making the best of yourself and creating a positive first impression. This chapter examines some of the techniques that can be adopted to achieve this:

♦ creating a positive first impression
  – visibly (face to face)
  – invisibly (by the written word or telephone)

♦ being interviewed for a job

♦ self-management
  – using time
  – building confidence

One-on-one situations are good for cutting your assertive teeth. You can try out new approaches and develop new skills in fairly safe circumstances. If you are with a trusted friend you can ask for feedback to get an idea of how you are doing. When you move into the public domain and become more visible, however, you will need to turn up the level of your assertive behavior and move from the subtle to the bold. More about this in Chapter 5.

In order to create a good first impression, you will need to manage the perceptions of others. This may be accomplished through the persona you project—which may, of course, be radically different from the one you revert to in private. This is fine as long as you are happy to handle the pluralism.

CREATING A POSITIVE FIRST IMPRESSION—VISIBLY

The first opportunity we have to create a good impression is at an initial meeting or during an interview for a job.

Human beings are incredibly judgmental. We generally look for similarities in those we are meeting for the first time because this reinforces us as individuals and gives us common ground to explore. We are less tolerant of those who take views diametrically opposed to ours or who live by a different set of values.

When meeting someone for the first time, you can be absolutely sure that the person has this lightning ability, as you do, to sum you up in something under ten seconds and be utterly convinced that her powers of perception are completely accurate! You have only these very few seconds, therefore, to create the impression of your choice.

Very often our first impressions are proved wrong in the long run. However, it does take an inordinate amount of time to dismantle a first impression and substitute for it a more accurate one.

Let us now examine some of the many factors that go into creating a first impression:

◆ appearance

◆ size, mobility, and national origin

◆ handshake

◆ gait, body language

◆ voice, accent, speech pattern, speech impediment, tone, and so on

Judgments are made on a combination of some or all of the above factors before a person says anything of consequence.

We will look at these factors one by one.

APPEARANCE

In order to decide *how* to make your impression, you must first determine *what* impression you wish to create. An obvious point, perhaps, but on that is often neglected.

Here are some factors to consider when planning your impact:

◆ the culture of the target organization

◆ the nature of the job

◆ the image you wish to create with your clothes
  - *bright colors can be overpowering*
  - *style can be appropriate/conventional/unconventional*
  - *accessories—shoes, ties, scarves, hairstyle, hair color, jewelry,*
    bags, belts, and briefcases all contribute to the overall impression

If you decide to create the image of a nonconformist—beware. Although this gives you greater freedom and enormous scope for painting a very individualistic picture, it is a high-risk strategy, especially in a conventional environment. The question to ask yourself is: How seriously do I want this job?

SIZE, MOBILITY, AND NATIONAL ORIGIN

There is very little most of us can do about our size, degree of mobility, or origin. Unfortunately, it is undeniable that these factors strongly influence a first impression, so be aware of them and quickly remove any concern that the interviewer may have.

If you think that you may encounter some form of prejudice, be proud and be direct. This is very disarming and will soon put the issue (if any) into the background, leaving you with the upper hand. It will also create a relaxed atmosphere for further discussion. This is an essential step to take if there is any possibility that the interviewer will perceive a physical barrier to your suitability for the job. Deal with likely issues honestly and without apology, then move on.

Here are some examples that illustrate how an interviewee can remove prejudice at the outset:

"Although you can see I am very large, I would like to reassure you that this does not hinder my performance."

"I would like you to know that my physical restrictions have enabled me to develop other skills to an extremely high level."

In the United States, certain laws protect individuals from the effects of prejudice on the basis of size, age, and looks, as well as of color, race, and creed. It is a sad indictment of human society that we have to go to these lengths to protect those that fall outside the norm.

HANDSHAKE
Within the first split second of meeting someone for the first time, we are there, proffering our hand as the best etiquette has taught us.

There are many varieties of handshake, some desperately disconcerting, others, businesslike and almost unremarkable.

The conclusions we draw from a handshake are out of all proportion to its significance. However, getting it wrong puts a large obstacle in the way of creating a good impression.

We have all experienced the limp handshake, the end-of-fingers handshake, the ferocious bone-breaker, the sweaty handshake, and the won't-let-go handshake.

The model way to shake someone's hand is to:

◆ offer an open hand, your palm facing toward the other's palm

◆ look the other party in the eye and smile

◆ take a firm hold of the person's hand and shake it up and down once or twice (no more)

◆ release (if you are going to wipe, wipe discretely)

GAIT, BODY POSITIONING

Body language is dealt with in great detail in Chapter 6, but while we are on the subject of first impressions, it is necessary to touch on the matter here.

The way in which you enter a room, move towards a greeting, walk, or sit all affects the first impression.

Assertive behavior can also be demonstrated nonverbally in the following three ways:

1. moving assertively (including the handshake)

2. sitting assertively

3. the quality or sound of the voice (not words)

Moving assertively: when preparing to enter a room, knock firmly on the door and wait for a response. Once you have been told to come in, open the door fully, step in and close the door behind you. Walk confidently into the room towards the greeting, with your hand ready.

Don't be timid. If you tap lightly on the door, no one will hear you. Then you will probably be anxious and uncertain—you have sabotaged yourself.

If you creep around the door, hug the wall and shuffle hesitantly towards the greeting, you will appear insipid and lacking in confidence. This is typical passive behavior. However, if you stride in, throw your briefcase down and sit without being invited to do so, it will not appear confident, as you hope, but aggressive.

Sitting assertively: sit straight and lean slightly forward. This gives the impression of meeting someone part way on his territory and makes you look interested and enthusiastic.

If you slouch or lean back with your bottom on the edge of the chair, you will appear uninterested and disrespectful.

If you huddle in your chair with your toes pointing together and your hands gripped firmly between your knees, you will look child-like and helpless.

Voice: there are many dimensions to your voice, most of which are difficult to control, such as a national or regional accent, a speech impediment or the quality of your voice.

Some of the vocal properties that you can control are the clarity of your speech, the pitch, the tone, and the speed of delivery.

The words you use, the grammatical patterns you choose when constructing your sentences, and the way you reinforce what you are saying with your hands all have a direct bearing on how you will be perceived, albeit unconsciously. More of this later.

CREATING A POSITIVE FIRST IMPRESSION—INVISIBLY

Our first contact with a person may be by letter, often accompanied by a résumé or curriculum vitae (CV), or on the telephone.

Because these modes of communication are stripped of the normally abundant visible information such as appearance, style, movement, and, in the case of the written word, voice, it becomes all the more important to make the most of what is left. These remote modes of communication are still filled with opportunities to create a good first impression.

We will look at the potential of these forms of communication in turn.

LETTER

There are significant advantages to making your first impression by letter. When initial contact is made through the written word, you have the luxury of time to plan the impression you wish to create.

Listed below are some useful tips on how to create a good impression by letter.

◆ Ensure that the quality of the paper and the appearance of the writing is excellent—no spelling mistakes, colloquialisms, or bad grammar.

◆ Typed or word-processed letters look the best, so use one of these methods if you can. Handwritten letters may do in some cases if you write attractively and legibly. Many bad characteristics are associated with poor handwriting.

◆ Make sure that what you have to say is succinct. Any information that you give in addition to what is necessary should be carefully chosen. It will reveal what is most significant to you and will say something about your priorities. At best, this could benefit you enormously, particularly if you have done your research properly.

CURRICULUM VITAE (CV)

A curriculum vitae emphasizes professional qualifications and activities. A CV is used primarily in academic circles. It's not unusual for this form of biographical statement to fill three to ten pages.

RESUME

People engaged in business and commerce expect to see your résumé. It's a short document designed to demonstrate qualifications for a particular job or position. Think of it as a one- or two-page sales letter describing your experience and competence.

Some people have a variety of résumés from which they choose for different purposes. Each one emphasizes an aspect of their past experience that is relevant to the job in question.

Some employers ask a job candidate for a professional summary. In this case, both a CV and a résumé would be submitted.

TELEPHONE

When communicating by telephone, you have the luxury of being invisible so you can get really comfortable with yourself and what you plan to say.

Here are some helpful tips on making a good first impression using the telephone:

◆ Smile when your call is answered; this can be detected.

◆ Use a pleasant greeting and state your name and purpose clearly.

◆ Plan what you are going to say (writing down key words will ensure you cover all the essential points).

◆ If you are trying to get your thoughts together, pace around if it helps and use gestures.

◆ If you are interrupted during your call, explain what has happened so that your failing concentration does not appear rude or uninterested.

◆ Summarize and confirm all agreements verbally so that you can be sure you have understood the other person.

◆ Establish who will initiate the next contact; if you are anxious, take the responsibility for this yourself.

◆ Follow up a telephone conversation with a letter of confirmation.

◆ If you seem to be listening for a long time, acknowledge what is being said by using terms like "aha," "mmmm," and "yes." Long silences can sound as if you are no longer there or have stopped paying attention.

◆ If you find you need to be assertive, stand up while talking on the telephone; it helps convey a feeling of strength.

ASSERTIVE INTERVIEWING SKILLS

Many books have been written on the subject of the interview. However, this section would not be complete without some reference to listening skills, open questions, and responding appropriately to questions—all of which are vital tools to wield when being interviewed. Chapter 6 explores the use of body language to develop rapport.

During a professionally conducted interview, the interviewer should talk for 5–10 percent of the time. Ideally, therefore, you have the remainder of the time to give as much relevant information about yourself as possible.

Your résumé or curriculum vitae will have conveyed all the professional, technical, and experiential information necessary to determine your suitability for the post. The interview is primarily geared towards finding out whether you will fit into the culture of the organization and work effectively with the rest of the team.

You will be prompted to give information about yourself through open questions.

Listen carefully for these because they provide you with the opportunity to show yourself in a good light. Examples of open questions are:

◆ *What* made you decide to . . . ?

◆ *How* would you tackle . . . ?

◆ *Explain* more about how you . . . and so on.

They are open-ended because you determine the content and limits of the answer; there are no bounds to them. They give you a wide scope to talk about your approach and your achievements. Closed questions, for comparison, might be:

◆ How long did you work for . . . ?

◆ How many staff were you responsible for at . . . ?

◆ When did you pass your driving test?

◆ Did you like working there?

These questions prompt short, defined responses and, as a consequence, the interviewer has to work extremely hard to extract sufficient information from you to reach a decision.

If you happen to be at an interview where the interviewer asks you closed questions, take the initiative and open them up yourself, saying something like:

◆ "Yes, I enjoyed being an apprentice *because* it gave me an opportunity to . . ."

◆ "I worked for Acme Corp. for ten years and thoroughly enjoyed it *because* it developed my ability to . . ."

Remember, do some basic research on the organization and the nature of its business before you attend an interview. Interviewers often ask, "What do you know about this organization?" You can easily impress them with a knowledgeable response to this question.

SELF-MANAGEMENT

USING TIME

It has long been claimed that time marches on inevitably in small, measured steps. Time is based on the natural frequency of the element cesium. Indeed, there is a cesium clock in Paris that acts as a time reference point for the entire world. We are obsessed with time.

It is a bold step, you may think, to step outside the belief system harbored by many eminent scientists and dispute the properties of this phenomenon called time, but step outside it we shall. We will learn to bend it, move it, expand and contract it—all in the presence of clear, heartfelt objectives.

Surely, we must all share the experience of having had a million and one things to do, believing that it was not humanly possible to complete them, yet found that we were sitting down at the end of the day with everything done and time enough for a cup of tea.

The secret of expanding time is having:

◆ *vision*—a clear understanding of what needs to be done

◆ *a plan*—a prioritized list of tasks to execute

◆ *method*—a knowledge of how to execute the tasks

◆ *impetus*—a determination or motivation to accomplish everything on the list

You will be able to identify these characteristics or skills in the high achievers in your organization. Why not adopt it for yourself?

Look out for time warps too. They usually happen when we are in the midst of a pleasant experience, like a vacation. At the time it feels endless; but when you return home, it feels as if it happened in a different lifetime. It's rather like watching a balloon drifting towards you: as it approaches, it looks as if it is traveling really slowly; however, when it moves on past you, it takes on the properties of a meteor and disappears at the speed of light.

We can either court this phenomenon or reject it.

To court it, extract the most pleasure out of every moment and completely absorb yourself in the task.

To reject it, keep returning to the problems.

As managers, or in our personal lives, the truth is that when we are focused, determined, and clear, time will allow us the space we need to achieve all that we wish. Give no room to negativity or doubt and you can be sure that the time will be there.

The opposite is also true, of course. When you are bored, dissipated, and uninspired, an hour can feel like aeons.

Phrases like "Well, you'll just have to make time!" are based on truth, however much we may resent it. Busy people make time all the time.

Time is only a question of perception. We must unlearn our conditioning; it is limiting us.

BUILDING CONFIDENCE

To conclude this chapter, let us look at what creating a positive image is all about: *confidence*.

By adopting some of the techniques and attitudes in this chapter, you will soon begin to trust that you are capable of forming and maintaining an image that pleases you. Initially, one small success is all you can ask for yourself. Having this safely behind you will be the beginning of building confidence. Start with something you find relatively easy, and move on to greater things from there.

Good habits, firmly established, are soon drawn into the subconscious. When you have progressed this far, you will find that your confidence level has increased significantly. Confidence and a healthy self-esteem are priceless assets and, if you are not fortunate enough to possess them naturally, they are well worth working for.

A positive mental attitude is key. Many managers have learned this from the experience of athletes who develop their minds as well as their bodies. Belief in yourself, coupled with professional expertise, will ensure your success.

Chapter 5

Being Assertive in the Public Arena

Chapter 4 looked at ways of creating a positive impression in one-on-one situations: at a job interview, on the telephone, and through writing.

This chapter explores how to develop this transient first impression into a durable professional image. To this end, we will concentrate on your ability to communicate assertively in public, among work colleagues and customers. As you grow in professional stature, you will increasingly find yourself in situations where many pairs of eyes will be watching you. You will be visible to a wider public.

Much of the assertive behavior about to be described will be applicable to more than one arena. Here we will focus on four common situations in which your ability to communicate assertively will reap great rewards:

◆ meetings

◆ negotiations

◆ presentations

◆ on-the-spot interviews

MEETINGS

Meetings are often dominated by the most aggressive members of the group. In these circumstances, passive attendees can feel completely overtaken by events because they feel unable to interject and make their points. Passive types often revert to passive/aggressive behavior on such occasions—deafeningly loud body language and more than a few sighs—or they become silent and resign themselves to the decisions made without their input.

A good chairperson ensures that a meeting is properly orchestrated and that everyone is given the opportunity to contribute. Often this leadership is sadly lacking, however, and meetings either take on the air of a battlefield or wander off the point and waste a lot of time—a common complaint.

For the purposes of illustrating how to handle meetings assertively, we will look at the worst scenario: that of a disorganized gathering dominated by one or two aggressive types. We will pepper this image with a few passive and passive/aggressive characters who are nursing hidden agendas.

After a few words on how to prepare for a meeting, we will pull this scenario apart and look at each component individually.

◆ assertive vs. aggressive

◆ assertive vs. passive/aggressive

◆ assertive vs. passive

◆ assertive vs. hidden agenda

PREPARING FOR A MEETING

Before attending a meeting, make sure that you have a copy of the agenda and that you fully understand why the meeting has been called.

Take with you all the supporting information you are likely to need. If you are not clear why a particular item has been included on the agenda, ask beforehand.

Make sure you know where the meeting is being held and get there on time. You will lose credibility if you turn up late, confused, or ill-prepared, and it will then be much harder to make an assertive and constructive contribution.

ASSERTIVE VS. AGGRESSIVE

Let's start by dealing with the aggressive component of the meeting.

Aggressive behavior often works in the short term. It intimidates and controls those who fear it, and many do. However, it is not worth adopting aggressive behavior as a long-term strategy. Eventually colleagues will get angry. The lack of regard and respect that the aggressive person exhibits will eventually lead to uncooperative and undermining responses. Once commitment has been lost, there is no way forward for the aggressor.

The use of assertive behavior in these circumstances can, however, draw the aggressor towards a healthier realm of communication. Here's how.

When faced with aggressive behavior, be calm, breathe deeply, and know that others at the meeting will be gunning for you. One word of caution, however: assertive behavior is about taking responsibility for yourself, not for others; so don't speak for the group, speak for yourself. Use "I" language.

You may have to field anger, criticism, and insults before you can start taking control of the communication. Remember though, aggressive behavior is weak behavior. Be confident; you *can* handle it.

Here is a checklist for dealing with aggressive behavior:

◆ Be calm; listen carefully.

◆ Take a deep breath and look for an opportunity to speak. If you need to interrupt, try to catch the speaker's eye and indicate your wish to contribute. If the speaker is determined to avoid eye contact, call her name politely and state your intention to contribute.

◆ Match the volume of your interruption to the volume of the speaker's voice.

◆ Once you have successfully entered the dialogue, acknowledge what has just been said, then lead off with an "I" statement. For instance: "I understand the point you are making, but I feel we could achieve more by . . ."

◆ If you are dismissed, repeat your comment in a different way. Repeat yourself assertively until you have been heard.

◆ Once you have the floor you may find you need to halt a return play interruption. In this case, raise your hand to signal stop. Using the person's name increases the power of your gesture.

◆ Summarize and confirm your understanding of a point or agreement before moving on.

◆ If you have not succeeded in making your point, register the fact. For example: "I know that you are eager to cover a lot of ground in this meeting, but I still feel . . ."

◆ Maintain dignity even if you are frustrated and reassert yourself on a later occasion. Persistence really does win in the end and you will become more effective each time you attempt assertive behavior.

ASSERTIVE VS. PASSIVE/AGGRESSIVE

Passive/aggressive behavior is reluctant-victim behavior. It attempts to be manipulative. A person may be angry with himself for giving away his power, so he does it with a bad attitude. This type of behavior causes bad atmospheres, resentment, embarrassment, and confusion. Often, one thing is said but the message is completely different. For instance:

Manager: Our best customer has just placed an urgent order, would you mind processing it immediately?

Sales Assistant (sarcastically): No, that's fine, I have all the time in the world!

Passive/aggressive behavior is thinly disguised. In a meeting a person may exhibit it through overt body language—rolling the eyes heavenward, exaggerated shifting in the chair, or impatient tapping with a pen.

Here are some ideas for dealing with passive/aggressive behavior:

◆ Expose the hidden message, whether verbal or nonverbal. For example: "I see that you are feeling negatively about this, would you mind discussing your objection?"

◆ Ask for the person's thoughts on the topic of obvious dispute.

◆ Listen actively and respond.

The passive/aggressive person has several options when her behavior is exposed. She can rise to the challenge and redeem herself; deny sending the message in the first place claiming that you are paranoid; or get defensive. The first option is obviously the best strategy; the latter two will only diminish their standing in others' eyes.

ASSERTIVE VS. PASSIVE

Passive behavior attempts to engender feelings of sympathy in others. It is as manipulative as passive/aggressive behavior but it pretends to be virtuous. Martyrs are classic passive types; all very laudable, but rather unpalatable. Passive people have very little self-respect, they do not stand up for themselves and are frightened to say no and be rejected.

A distinguishing characteristic of a passive person is the use of silence. This can sometimes go on for a very long time and usually covers up running dialogue in his mind that is victim based ("Why are you picking on me?" "I wish you would shut up and leave me out of this!").

Dealing with a passive person is not dissimilar to handling the passive/aggressive approach. First, expose his abdication:

"I am not clear where you stand on this issue, would you tell me what your feelings are?" (Note the use of the "I" statement and the open question, *what*?)

Match silence with silence. It takes an *extremely* passive person to remain mute in the teeth of a silent and expectant gaze, especially if everyone at the meeting is engaged in the same tactic. Once he starts to talk, use your active listening skills to encourage the flow.

However, if you lose patience with his silence, repeat your comment or try a different approach if you think this will help. If you get to a point of exasperation, inform the passive person that you will have to deduce his feelings if he is not prepared to share them and that you will have to proceed according to your deductions. Invite him to support you in your course of action.

ASSERTIVE VS. HIDDEN AGENDA

You will inevitably come across people who play their cards very close to their chests, especially in organizations where internal politics are prominent. In these cultures, people are always on the defensive, protecting themselves from exploitation or disadvantage. Sometimes this fear is imaginary, sometimes it is real, but whatever the cause, you will need common techniques to deal with it.

You will probably be able to identify the political animals among your colleagues because their behavior will appear inconsistent. They will apparently change their opinions or approach without reason, leaving a trail of confusion and uncertainty behind them. Once this erratic style has caught your attention, look at the interplay of circumstances and try to identify the likely political, and usually personal, gain that is being sought. You may then be close to the real motivation of those people.

Significant coincidences that benefit one individual do not usually occur without some help. Look for coincidences, therefore, and identify the beneficiaries. Coupled with hindsight, the hidden agenda may suddenly be revealed to you and past, previously confusing, behaviors will fall into context. This knowledge is useful; it is power. Do not try to tackle the individual. Hidden agendas, by their very nature, can always be denied and you will end up looking paranoid or foolish.

It is probably worth testing your theory by predicting the likely reaction of your colleague in certain circumstances. If, when these circumstances occur, your prediction proves correct, the hidden agenda is likely to be what you suspected. If not, think again; maybe you *are* paranoid!

Having understood a colleague's private motivation, you will have a clear picture of where you fit into the pattern of things. This will enable you to plan your approach. This could be one of avoidance, of course, if you choose not to get caught up in the politics of the organization; or it may be a strategic option—the choice is yours.

Here is a checklist for identifying a hidden agenda:

◆ Examine coincidences that benefit one person, or a specific group of people.

◆ Look for inconsistent behavior: this may take the form of an unlikely relationship, nonverbal messages, or a sudden and inexplicable abdication of responsibility.

◆ Put your observations into context using hindsight; this may help you identify the hidden agenda.

◆ Test your theory as innocuously and as anonymously as possible.

◆ It is probably best to keep this testing to yourself.

◆ If you are going to tackle someone on her private agenda, be absolutely sure of your ground and that you can handle it in the most assertive way possible. Some tips on this were given in the passages dealing with passive/aggressive or purely passive behavior.

◆ Look for a motivation: if you are suddenly flavor of the month with someone who is known to be ambitious, ask yourself why.

◆ Be vigilant. It is always possible that a hidden agenda is being worked out somewhere within your organization.

NEGOTIATIONS

There are some very simple rules for conducting yourself effectively and assertively in negotiations.

Negotiations can fall into several categories. First, there are those taking place in the working environment with one other person such as your boss, a colleague, or a member of your staff. Moving up in scale, the boardroom often witnesses negotiations among several colleagues whose views reside in different camps. Then there are those conducted between two opposing parties. When these two parties cannot agree, they may resort to the services of an arbitrator or mediator.

Whatever the situation, whether it is simple problem solving or a full-scale meeting between managers and a trade union, the basic rules for successful negotiating are the same. More often than not, it is merely a question of scale.

Here are the basic steps for negotiating successfully:

◆ Know exactly what you wish to achieve and be absolutely clear on the level of your authority.

◆ Be assertive and use positive body language.

◆ Make sure you understand the other's viewpoint.

◆ Convey your own viewpoint clearly and state your desired outcome.

◆ Look for areas of common ground to reinforce mutual interests and to develop a commitment to a satisfactory resolution.

◆ Listen actively and demonstrate understanding throughout the discussion.

◆ Never bluff, fudge, manipulate, or lie.

◆ Never offer something you cannot deliver.

◆ If you are feeling pressured, ask for a recess.

◆ Communicate your proposals clearly and concisely and establish those of the other party.

◆ Summarize the areas of difference and explore the extent of these; identify the issues where compromise is possible.

◆ Having distilled the main area of contention, discuss any concessions that you are both prepared to make.

◆ Summarize and confirm your agreement in writing.

PRESENTATIONS

Presentations strike fear into the hearts of most managers, whatever their seniority. They are one of the most visible and exposed professional platforms and can leave your image enhanced, intact, or in tatters.

Usually you will have advance warning of the requirement to make a presentation and will also, therefore, have time to prepare and practice for the occasion.

These two points are most important: *prepare* and *practice*.

Those who are naturals at making presentations are the exception rather than the rule. Most good presenters are only good because they have invested time in preparation and practice. Everyone can do it if they try and everyone *can* enjoy the experience.

There is nothing more satisfying than the flow of success when you step down from the platform having made an excellent presentation. It really is worth investing the time and energy to get it right.

Of course, much has been written on presentation skills, and clearly justice cannot be done to the subject in a few short paragraphs. However, here are a few pointers to help you add this mode of communication to the assertiveness resources you are assembling.

PREPARATION AND PRACTICE

◆ Make sure you understand the purpose of the presentation.

◆ Have a clear impression of your audience, their level of intelligence, and their expectations; this will enable you to pitch your presentation correctly.

◆ Prepare your talk:
 Beginning—Tell them what you are going to say
 Middle—Say it
 End—Tell them what you have said
 (Most people will only retain about three points)

◆ Prepare visual aids:
 Overhead projector slides—These should *add* to your presentation; they should be bold, clear, and *never* more than a paragraph.
 Handouts—These can contain more detailed information along with copies of your overhead slides. They should be top quality.
 35mm slides—Not always an advantage as you have to make your presentation in a darkened room. Not everyone can handle technology competently, either. If you do use them, they should be clear and concise.

◆ Prepare a set of cards with keyword prompts, facts, or difficult names on them to help you if you are nervous.

• Practice in front of a mirror, colleagues, friends, and family. Make sure you get the timing right and get this audience to fire awkward questions at you.

MAKING THE PRESENTATION

◆ Wear clean, comfortable, and conservative clothes. If you don't, your audience will pay more attention to your attire than to what you have to say.

◆ Arrive in plenty of time; familiarize yourself with the equipment and check that your slides are in the right order.

◆ Make sure you have a glass of water handy in case your mouth dries up.

◆ If you are using torch pointers, telescopic pointers, or infrared remote controls, practice beforehand.

◆ Relax, by whatever means suit you.

◆ Tell your audience what you expect from them in terms of inter-ruptions, discussion, or questions; you may prefer to take these as you go along, or leave them to the end.

◆ Enjoy your talk but remain vigilant: it is too easy to be drawn into letting your guard down and saying something contentious. If you cannot answer a question, be honest about it and tell the questioner that you will find out and get back to them.

◆ Don't tell jokes that may offend someone. When in doubt, leave it out!

◆ Don't talk down to your audience, but equally, don't assume they understand the technicalities of your subject.

◆ Pause from time to time. This is a performance, and pauses are useful for dramatic effect—and to collect your thoughts.

◆ Of course, *use assertive language and body posture.*

◆

ON-THE-SPOT INTERVIEWS

Today, more and more managers are required to field questions from the media. It may only be a matter of time before a journalist ferrets you out and asks you some questions about some aspect of your business. Whether you are subjected to a hostile interview or a friendly one, the experience can be awesome—especially if there are lights, a camera crew, and so on.

Commonly, now, chief executives are trying to project a more approachable image through acquainting themselves with individual members of their organizations. Increasingly, too, organizations are being encouraged to take responsibility for developing a two-way relationship with the communities in which their organizations belong. These new trends will lead towards much greater public awareness and interest in your business.

When approached by an interviewer or journalist, you may feel very exposed. However, here are some guidelines for dealing with this experience.

First, *don't panic* (this one is easy if you are now fully assertive and confident).

Second, remember, if someone wants information from you, *you hold the power*. Unless he is prepared to floor you, he will have to wait until you are ready to deliver.

Third, if you are unsure of what you want to say, ask for time to consider your response. If the questioner is persistent, smile, repeat your need for time, acknowledge his position, and explain that you would rather assemble accurate information before responding.

Beware: If a journalist starts getting chatty with you after the interview and asks for your opinion on a contentious matter, watch out; you may think that the interview has ended, but it hasn't.

TAKING STOCK OF PROGRESS

By now you should have started to gather some useful tools for developing your assertive skills. You may have had a chance to practice some of these techniques and found that they really work. These early successes should increase your confidence and fire your enthusiasm to learn more, take control, and have the courage to set your own goals.

Chapter 6

Body Language

This chapter explains some of the forms of body language that have the most impact on others. This is by no means an exhaustive study of the subject, but it will maximize the effect you can create when you communicate assertively.

The chapter focuses on these areas:

◆ assertive body language

◆ use of gestures

◆ developing rapport

◆ use of verbal language

◆ interpreting body language

Your body really can speak louder than words.

ASSERTIVE BODY LANGUAGE

Because your body conveys such a large proportion of what you are communicating, it is worth concentrating on this area for a short time and considering what it is we convey with our bodies and how we can be sabotaged by them.

Body watching is a useful exercise—but try to be discreet. You will notice that when two people are engrossed in riveting conversation,

they are completely unaware of their bodies. (Unless the conversation is about sex of course; in these circumstances we are not subtle.) We use our bodies at the unconscious level, therefore, to emphasize points or to transmit secondary messages.

Assertive behavior is distinguished by the continuity between the verbal and the nonverbal. In other words, your body reflects precisely what you are saying when you are in an assertive mode.

Try saying "Look over there" without using some part of your body to point. Indeed, you could draw someone's attention to something without using words at all, only gestures. This is a crude example of the power of body language, but it serves to illustrate that we are driven to use it, and, what's more, it is the dominant channel of communication.

Just think how obvious it can be when you are nervous. Your body will communicate this rather than the message you are trying to transmit verbally.

The primary vehicle for body language is emotion. Control your emotions and you will be able to control your messages. Try not to go to extremes, though.

To start being body aware, therefore:

◆ Body watch (without staring too obviously).

◆ Ask for feedback from your colleagues and friends on your use of body language.

◆ Have an imaginary conversation in front of the mirror (very embarrassing at first, but you will get used to it) and see if you can identify the way you use gestures and the amount of gestures you use.

We will touch briefly on the most potent aspects of body language.

◆ space

◆ stance

◆ touch

SPACE

We all carry with us an egg-shaped exclusion zone that varies in size in direct proportion to our circumstances, purpose, and level of comfort. As a point of interest, you can usually measure the size of someone's egg by the length of their focal attention. On a train, this is almost zero (people often look glazed or they focus on reading matter); at work it can extend to include one person or a small gathering of people; at a large presentation, it can reach to the extremities of an entire hall.

Mostly, varying the size of the egg is an instinctive part of our behavior. However, it can be very useful to understand the nature of personal space so that it can be used to good effect.

Learning point 1: *If we do not include people in our personal space, it is impossible to influence them.*

Notice how you shut down when someone you dislike comes too close, or someone you're not sure about comes too close too soon. I'm sure we have all experienced backing away from someone as they repeatedly trespass on our personal territory until the next step takes us through the window or into a cupboard.

Remember, too, a time when you were part of a vast audience, and the presenter or entertainer made you feel as if you were the only person in the room. This was because they extended their personal space to include you.

Notice how you use your space, and how you act differently with family, colleagues, and those in authority. As an exercise, practice drawing your space in until its boundaries meet your body. Then try filling a room with your presence by expanding your space. You can do this by changing the point of your focal and conscious attention. Accompany this with a visualization of yourself as either completely invisible or extraordinarily influential.

Learning point 2: *The more space you use, the more impact you will have.*

Naturally tall people have an advantage because, by definition, they occupy a large amount of space. Yet these people are often shy and withdrawn by nature. Perhaps they are this way because they do not have the confidence to handle their natural authority.

Short people, however, can make up for their lack of size by adopting a good assertive style, and indeed, a large number of short people have been extraordinarily successful. Unfortunately, however, their communication style sometimes overcompensates for their lack of physical stature and becomes aggressive.

There are ways, however, of sitting and standing that look big and carry huge impact. By adopting some of the following techniques, short people can actually grow in others' perceptions.

Here are some techniques for creating presence:

Assertive standing: stand straight and think tall. Try not to twine your legs around each other or stand with your weight on one leg.

Nothing destroys the image like crumpling onto the floor because you have overbalanced!

When you wish to communicate powerfully, again, stand straight, feet planted firmly on the floor, body centered, hands at your side. If it is hard to push you over physically, it will be hard to push you around verbally.

Assertive sitting: convey confidence by using as much space as possible while sitting. Sit with your body at an angle, well back in the chair and place your arms on the armrests. Sit small and you will be perceived as small.

STANCE

Your posture conveys a huge impression, so it is important to get it right.

Everyone notices someone who stands upright and walks well. This is a good habit to cultivate. It portrays confidence and authority.

Tall people are notorious for stooping and they always say it is because they can't get through the doors. However, it is an enviable gift to be tall; many would give their eye teeth for height—so, if you are tall, duck only when necessary. Stoop when you are young and you will have no choice but to stoop when you are old.

Short people can walk tall too. In fact, people of under five foot three can look six foot tall if they stand proud. We often confuse confidence for size, so you can make the most of this misconception by cultivating your personal stature.

TOUCH

Taking the liberty to touch people conveys superiority. A boss can pat his staff on the back, but they would probably feel uncomfortable reciprocating this action. A pat on the back is an authoritative action. If it remains unchallenged, a hierarchy is established.

A good way of putting things back on an even footing is to look for an immediate opportunity to touch them back. You might say, "Excuse me," as you pick a hair off their jacket, or say, "You've brushed up against some dust," as you sweep their chest briskly with the back of your hand.

THE USE OF GESTURES

Gestures can either reinforce your communication or they can draw attention away from what you are saying. They should be used prudently, therefore, to maximize their effect.

Gestures include everything from windmill arms (sit on your hands if this is you) to almost imperceptible movements of the face, head, torso, or arms (they rarely involve the use of the legs).

The most common gestures are made with hands alone and they serve to emphasize what is being said by the mouth.

The type of gesture you choose to use can indicate something about your personality. If you prod the air more than artistically necessary, you will appear aggressive. Open gestures, arms out away from the body, can indicate an open and warm personality. Be too energetic and untidy with your movements and you will come across as fake and disorganized—especially if this is the style of your dress also. No gesturing looks passive.

Assertive gestures tend towards the moderate ground. Timing and relevance are crucial. They should flow smoothly and mirror as closely as possible what is being said.

DEVELOPING RAPPORT

Empathizing with another does not depend solely on the words you use. Much of the rapport is carried in your body language.

If you watch two people talking empathetically and unselfconsciously, you will probably notice that their bodies take on virtually the same demeanor. For example, both may have crossed their legs, put an elbow on the table, and their chin in the palm of their hands. If they are drinking, you will often find that the drinks diminish at exactly the same rate. They will have *matched* and *mirrored* each other's behavior. If you do this consciously, but subtly, you will find that your ability to build rapport will have improved greatly.

Should you find yourself in an unpleasant conversation and you wish to alleviate the tension, it is possible to do this also by matching and mirroring the other's body language. Having matched and held their body position for some time, you can start moving your own body towards a more relaxed position. You will soon find that they start mirroring you and the tension will fade. It is impossible to remain aggressive when you are physically relaxed.

Beware, though: if you are not sufficiently subtle in your mirroring and matching skills, it will look as if you are mimicking the other's behavior. If this is the impression you create, it will be very difficult to make amends.

Couple this technique with good eye contact, active listening skills, lots of head nods, "aha," "mmmm," and so on, and you will be able to build rapport with the best of them.

Being able to empathize with someone involves understanding her feelings by getting beneath the surface. This can often be achieved by being able to relate what she says to a similar experience of your own. If you are at sea, however, with no common understanding, the mirroring and matching technique can be used to engender the same feelings in you that are being experienced by the other person. If the other person has lost confidence, for instance, and takes on the fetal position, try it out for yourself and see what emotions it brings up. You will probably gain a better understanding of the person's feelings and be able to empathize more effectively.

THE USE OF VERBAL LANGUAGE

The words we choose and the way we construct sentences can assist us in the process of building rapport.

To illustrate this, think of the way we talk to children. We are constantly reflecting back to them the words they use themselves. The principle is the same here. Listen for the kind of words used by the person with whom you are trying to build rapport and reflect this style of language back to him.

A manager often uses a distinctive language that is related to the function or specialty of his or her role. Finance, information technology, manufacturing, design, and development all have their own languages. If you use the same language with these specialists, they will feel comfortable with your style. Use a different language, and they will feel alienated.

Here are some examples of language compatibility:

A financier's language includes words like: *balance*, *bottom line*, *assets*, *investments*, and *credit*.

Some of the following words would be used by an information technologist: *logical*, *image*, *capacity*, *network*, *hardware*, and *upgrade*.

The same sentence can be constructed differently for each audience.

To the financier: "On *balance*, I feel it would be to our *credit* . . ."

To the information technologist: "It would seem the most *logical* approach to *upgrade* our *image* by . . ."

And to a visionary designer whose language may include words like: *see*, *impact*, *style*, *color*, *create*, *proportion*, and *impression*: "I can *see* that we could *create* the best *impression* by . . ."

INTERPRETING BODY LANGUAGE
Beware: This is not an exact science.

When watching someone for the telltale signs of a hidden message, don't only engage your brain, engage your senses too. People often *think* that they are privy to the inner secrets of another person, but you have to be bordering on the telepathic to really *know*.

However, here are a few guidelines to interpreting body language.

Be aware of the environment in which you are making your observation. If it is cold, your subject may have a tense jaw or their arms may be folded tightly across their bodies. In these circumstances, they *may not* be either nervous or aggressive, but *they may*.

Watch for leakage. Leakage happens to someone who, say, is controlling her nerves, for all intents and purposes, extremely well. However, nerves have to exhaust themselves somewhere so watch for toes curling and uncurling at the end of shoes; muscles clenching and unclenching around the jaw, grinding teeth, rattling change in the pocket, and quivering knees. As resourceful human beings, we have many such outlets.

Mostly look for discontinuity and coincidence. If someone is pledging his unequivocal support but shaking his head as he does so, watch your back.

If someone says "I never lie" at the same time as moving her pointing finger from side to side, don't believe her. This is the gesture of denial; her body is denying the statement.

If someone says, "I am not interested in scoring points with the boss" and yet is coincidentally around the boss at the most politically charged moments, watch you don't get sideswiped.

Watch people's eyes. It sounds obvious to say that people look where their interest lies, but sometimes, during an unguarded moment, it is interesting to note exactly where this is—or who it is.

Sometimes it is easier to identify anti body language. People tend to be very clear when they dislike someone. You can see it in their eyes and in the way they move their bodies away from the object of their distaste. This is the opposite of mirroring. Sometimes their complete and habitual removal from the scene gives the game away.

When people like each other, they get into close proximity—into personal comfort zones. They may touch; they often have good and prolonged eye contact; they smile and reinforce and reflect each other's behavior. Sometimes you are aware of chemistry, when there are no identifiable body signals. It is interesting to observe this behavior and speculate on what it is that causes this effect.

SUMMARY

This chapter has merely skimmed the surface of a very powerful aid to communication. We have learned that the body will not lie for you. This makes your motivation visible, much more visible than you probably realize. However, you may now be more aware and may be able to body watch from a more informed position.

We have covered:

◆ how your body can help you be more assertive

◆ how to use gestures

◆ how to develop rapport using mirroring and matching

◆ the use of language

◆ developing a feel for the hidden message

Remember, your body (including voice—not words) and eyes carry about 90 percent of any message you are trying to convey. Because the proportion is so large, this aspect of communication has powerful potential. If you use your nonverbal knowledge skillfully, you will find that your level of control and your assertiveness will increase significantly.

Enjoy it.

Chapter 7

Personal Power

We have almost come full circle now, so to close the book's assertiveness training, we will discuss personal power—how to win it, how to hold it, and how to succeed with it.

The interesting thing about personal power is that you don't have to be born particularly advantaged to have it. It is not *dependent* upon your looks, size, intelligence, wealth, or talents. Some of these may help; but *anyone* can acquire power, be it political, professional, personal, or all three.

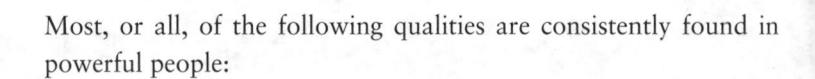

Most, or all, of the following qualities are consistently found in powerful people:

◆ clarity of vision

◆ well-defined values and beliefs

◆ confidence

◆ powerful communication

◆ an ability to build relationships

◆ political skill

Power remains only with those who respect it—abuse it at your peril. There may be a short-term gain for those who win power through confidence tricks, but it is inevitable that the fall from power will be in direct proportion to the con.

Let's take each element of personal power and examine it separately.

CLARITY OF VISION

It is essential to create a framework upon which you can hang your power. It is only when you know where you are going and are 100 percent committed to getting there that you can plan the way forward to your success. It doesn't matter which path you take, or whether you change the route from time to time, as long as you keep your eye on the goal.

Identifying the goal in the first place does require vision. Once you have this—and this is usually acquired through self-knowledge—the rest will fall into place.

If you have difficulty establishing your primary goal, start with a series of smaller ones. These will soon form a pattern that will lead you towards an understanding of what you wish to achieve. Ask yourself where you would like to be in 10, 20, or 50 years' time. Will maintaining your present course and direction bring you long-term satisfaction? Don't be concerned if your goal is extraordinarily ambitious. All those who have succeeded started out with impossible dreams. Equally, don't be ashamed if your goal is not particularly ambitious. This may mean that you are meeting your needs extremely well and you are way ahead of the game.

Visionaries take the following steps to create a framework upon which they can build their successes.

They:

◆ identify personal goals

◆ see their goals clearly and imagine what it is like to have reached them

◆ make a commitment to achieve them by a certain time

◆ act as if their goals have already been achieved

If you don't put a time limit on the attainment of your goals, your mind will always think of them as being in the future. Acting as if you have already reached your goals helps to bring them into the present.

Test these steps for yourself. Start small to gain confidence in the process.

WELL-DEFINED VALUES AND BELIEFS

Know what you value and believe. This is really much more difficult than it appears because values and beliefs have a habit of changing to suit different circumstances. Dig deep though; these underpin all your behaviors.

In the process of getting to know your values and beliefs you will have to ask yourself certain questions like: What price are you prepared to pay for your success? Consider the following areas.

◆ *personally*—intimate relationships (partner, family, friends)

◆ *spiritually*—what you feel is right or wrong; what you need to do to feel good about yourself

◆ *professionally*—career progression, promotion

◆ *politically*—being in the right place at the right time

If you ask a powerful person the question, "What price are you prepared to pay for your success?" he will have a clear, well-thought-out answer that is right for him. He is absolutely comfortable living within the framework of his values and beliefs. Any conflict—and conflict develops from time to time as the balance of his life changes—is addressed in the light of this value set.

Powerful people are comfortable with themselves. It is almost tangible.

CONFIDENCE

Here, we get back to the basics of *successful assertiveness*. Respect and honor yourself. You are as worthy as the next person.

Self-worth is the precursor to building confidence. If you believe in yourself, others will too.

True confidence enables you to handle any situation with aplomb. Even in situations that you have not met before, you will be able to draw on your experience and extrapolate from your past behavior to meet the needs of the moment.

A sudden lack of confidence petrifies and paralyzes the mind; all coping mechanisms seem to miraculously disappear. This rapid evacuation of all that you have learned will undermine your attempts at building confidence and put you back at square one again. So be kind to yourself; know that these things happen to everybody and that you are still a worthy individual. Forgive what you perceive to be your mistakes and move on.

The more you practice assertive behavior, the less often sudden losses in confidence will happen. As with your goals (gaining confidence may be one of them, of course) try believing that you have already succeeded and act that way. It will soon become a reality.

POWERFUL COMMUNICATION

Powerful people are often extremely good communicators. Their communication skills are characterized by typical assertive behavior, and more.

Having a vision is not enough. The only way a vision becomes a reality is through motivating others to play their parts, and the only way to motivate is to communicate. Only in very rare cases are visions actualized in a vacuum; usually they are dependent upon someone, or many people, cooperating in some way.

Few of us are natural orators, but we can learn from those who are. Here are a few qualities that you can learn to develop in yourself.

◆ vision (remember Dr. Martin Luther King, Jr. and "I have a dream . . .")

◆ belief—in your purpose, your ability, and the ability of your team

◆ acute observation (listening, watching, sensing)

◆ ability to develop empathy

◆ ability to judge the mood of the moment and respond appropriately (flexibility/intuition)

◆ a sense of timing and theater

Powerful communicators regard their public appearances as theatrical performances. They create an impact, build tension, move their audience, and leave them on a high.

AN ABILITY TO BUILD RELATIONSHIPS

It is extremely difficult to build and maintain relationships at the best of times, but it is especially difficult when driven by the work environment. Nonetheless, this ability is crucial if you wish to rise to the top.

There is no magic formula for developing good relationships and they can be stamped with a variety of styles—friendly, nurturing, respectful, mysterious, controlling, aggressive, and so on. Try to identify your style and check out the impression you create with colleagues.

Professional relationships are often fraught with difficulty because they have to be developed with people who are imposed upon us, not chosen by us. Indeed, some of our colleagues we might actively avoid when we're out of the work environment. Building good relationships therefore demands patience, determination, and the ability to step back and see things from a different perspective.

Most people do not try to be bad or difficult. If this is the behavior they exhibit, it usually indicates that they hold a belief that is causing them distress. If you encounter this behavior as a manager, you may need to spend some time delving below the surface to weed out the problem. However, beware: you cannot merely go through the motions, and you may learn some unpalatable truths about yourself in the process.

Much can be done to maintain relationships remotely (by telephone, letter, or memo), but first you have to know and understand the people who work around you. This is usually done at times when the pressure is off or at times when the office socializes together. There is a fine line to tread between being too involved and too remote. You will have to determine the best balance for yourself; but remember that power-holders are often characterized by a certain amount of mystique.

A sobering thought to leave you with: People always remember your worst behavior and this dominates their impression of you. Bear this in mind when you feel you are about to lose your temper.

POLITICAL SKILL

Office politics is a minefield because the players are all working out their personal agendas. It is an intensely self-interested activity and difficult to identify because the motivation behind the actions of others is often unknown and conclusions about them are frequently pure speculation.

A good politician, however, can identify the game, the players, and the rules through careful observation. Some, but not many, are lucky enough to be instinctive in this arena. Derived theories can be tested by injecting dye to see where it reappears or by dangling bait to see who bites. This can be an extremely illuminating activity and sometimes the outcome is very surprising. Be warned, though: it can also be a dangerous game, as there are always more experienced players on the field.

Politics can be played up and down the organization and the position that you occupy on the hierarchy or your political dexterity determines your potential.

Controlling the way you are perceived by your colleagues is a fairly low-key political activity and you owe it to yourself to do this effectively—whatever your ambitions.

Learn what you can about the interests, circumstances, and ambitions of others within your organization and identify critical relationships. Keep an eye out for those with influence and promote yourself among these people.

You may have a role model or mentor in your organization whom you can study or learn from. Virtually all successful people can identify a person who influenced them strongly in this way and at whose feet they lay their success. Try to identify one for yourself.

Whatever you do, do it with comfort, courage, and conviction. The maverick approach may sound attractive, but it is an extremely risky strategy.

SUMMARY

This chapter touched upon the dominant features of *personal power*. The subject holds books' worth of potential and is a fascinating subject of study, but there is no room here to go into more detail. However, much can be understood and achieved by thinking through the points noted here and testing them out in your professional environment.

Having worked your way through these seven chapters, you should now have the basic tools to move forward as a successful and assertive professional.

Remember, successful assertiveness ultimately boils down to three main points:

◆ *Understand yourself* (values, beliefs, the whys and wherefores of your nature).

◆ *Know yourself* (wants, predispositions, ambitions, desires).

◆ *Value yourself* (confidence, rights).

From this position of knowledge, you will be well placed to make your choices—about how you wish to be perceived, how to plan your career, and how to create and manage your impression.

The path to becoming truly and effectively assertive is a rewarding one. Nothing is wasted and each small step builds towards greater and greater success. Don't give up, and don't lose sight of the fact that above all else, you are entitled to this amount of control over your life.

Good luck and enjoy being assertive.

INDEX